Dedication

Dedicated to my beloved children, Joshua & Jessica,
who inspired this project.

A very special thanks to my mother and father, for their
support throughout the entire process.
-M.S.

A heartfelt thanks to my brother, mother and father for
all they have done throughout my publishing career.
-D.D.C.

Dedicated to my loving father.
-R.D.

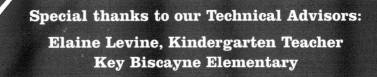

Special thanks to our Technical Advisors:

Elaine Levine, Kindergarten Teacher
Key Biscayne Elementary

Jean-Claude Misset, Music Teacher
Key Biscayne Elementary

Dr. Richard Rose, Professor of Music
Miami-Dade College, Commercial Music Department

Jane Pyle, Professor of Music Education
Miami-Dade College

Dr. Eugene A. Greco, Professor of Music
University of Miami

Gail Slatko
Reading Specialist
Miami-Dade County Public Schools

Mark Slatko
Senior Copywriter
Mark My Words, Inc.

Mr. James A. Smith, District Supervisor
Division of Life Skills & Special Projects
Music Education Program
Miami-Dade County Public Schools

Dr. Marcus D. Benedetto, Consultant

Cover Photograph by Joanne Williams, Inc. Designed by Dana Duane Craft

Special thanks to Raphael & Monica Lima, Marsh & Miosotys Smith,

Elena B. Rodriguez, Michael Oviedo, Camilo Palomeque, Espy Rodriguez,

Lester Carrodeguas, Phillip Church, Mabel Ledo, Mark Hart & Freddrick Jewkes

for their friendship, helpfulness and support

during the early stages of this product's development.

Additional thanks to Reiner & Reiner, P.A., Brian Root, Gene Cokeroft (The Suntones Quartet)

and his wife Iris, Joe Longo, Cliff Balestra, Laura Borrego, Carlos Alayeto, Karen Hoffman, Dave H

and Jay Love for their support along with the generous support of Ransom Everglades School.

Special thanks to our Executive Producers:
Keith V. Maling
Chdawan & Oscar, LLC
Jim "Bebop" Becker

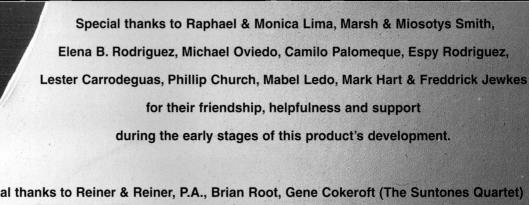

Produced by Grand Staff Musical Productions, LLC
Created, written and directed by Mike Singer
Designed & illustrated by Dana Duane Craft
Music by Robert Dante & Mike Singer
All instruments & voices performed by Robert Dante (Guitar-Mike Singer)
Additional voices by: Gaetano Contella, Southern Hightz, Laura Borrego, Carlos Alayeto, Mike Singer
"Father Time & Officer Bar Line" Rap written & performed by Robert Dante
"Grand Staff's Musical Party" Rap written & performed by Southern Hightz (Nacho Typical, Mike G. & J
Audio CD produced, engineered & mixed by Robert Dante @ Velvet Basement Studios, Miami, FL
Additional mixing by J-FLY
Mastered by Jose Blanco @ Master House Studios, Miami, FL

Audio CD

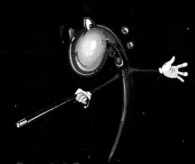

In the world of music there lives a
wise old musician known as Grand Staff.
He has ten lines on his body,
and a space in the middle divides them in half.

1

"I have five lines up top," he sings, "and five down below.
That's where all my musical friends like to go.
If you want to know about music, you need to know about me.
Because on my lines and spaces is where music will be!"

Grand Staff has many musical friends,
and he loves to make music with them.

Together they live on a piano, where they make music in a fun way.
You see, the piano has a musical keyboard that they all like to play!

"With our tiny instruments, little voices and musical keyboard,
we can play and sing Harmonies, Melodies, Scales and Chords."

5

One day Grand Staff decided to have a musical party.
So he began inviting his musical friends to come.

"We will sing and dance and make music together," he said.
"We will have lots and lots of fun!"

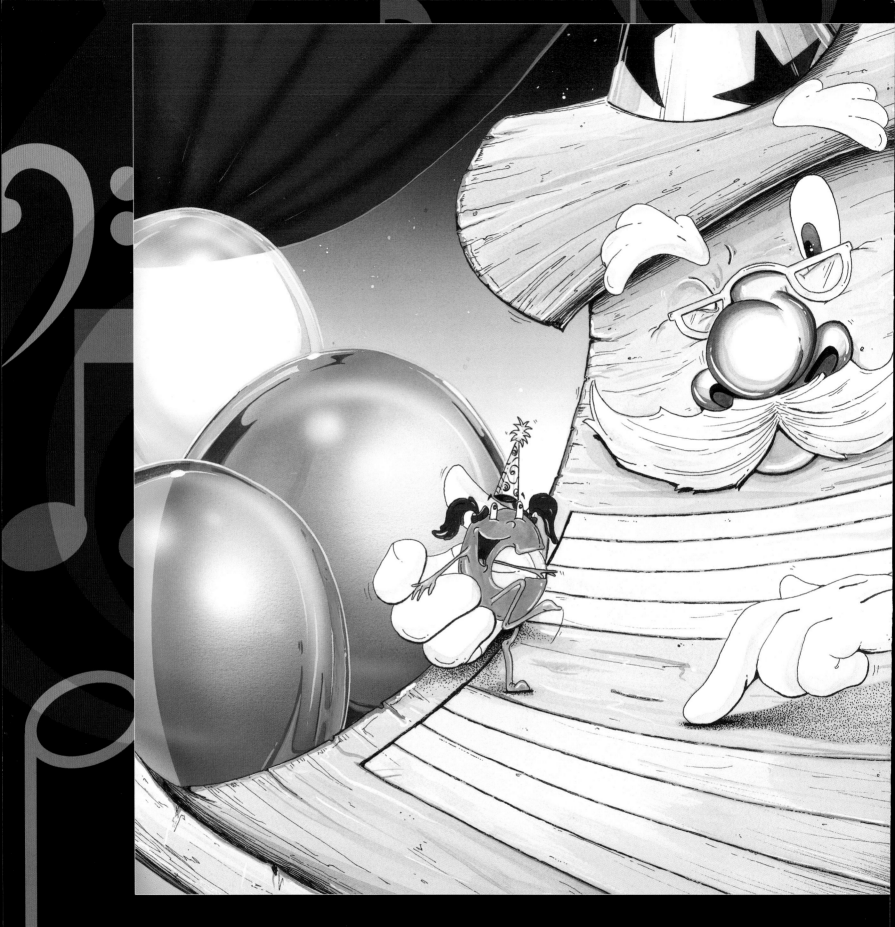

First he invited his best friend, Middle C,
who sat on Grand Staff on the line in-between.

"My name is Middle C.
When you're reading music this is where I will be.
On Grand Staff, on the line in-between,
dividing the lines up top from the lines below, you see!"

10

Next, Grand Staff invited the musical Clefs:
Mr. F Clef and Mrs. G Clef.

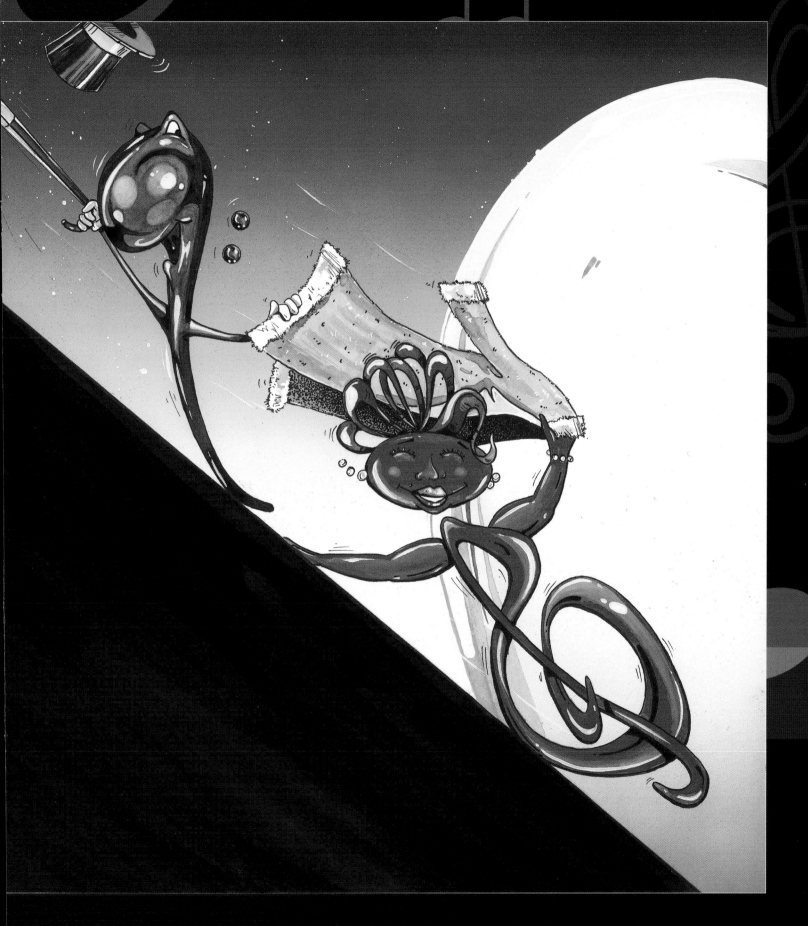

"Hurry, hurry! Let's not be late for this musical date!"
said Mr. F Clef as the Clefs hurried to the musical party.

When the Clefs arrived at the musical party scene,
Middle C jumped off of Grand Staff to dance and sing.

When you're playing the piano keys, in the middle of them is where I will be.
With low-pitched keys to the left of me and high-pitched keys to the right,
that's the part I'll play while making music with Grand Staff tonight!"

As the Clefs arrived at Grand Staff's side, Mr. F Clef sat low and Mrs. G Clef sat high.
"Since I have a high-pitched voice, I will sit up here and sing high.
Sol, la, ti, Do, re, mi, Fa, Sol!" sang Mrs. G Clef.
"Since I have a low-pitched voice, I will sit down here and sing low.
Fa, mi, re, Do, ti, la, Sol, Fa!" sang Mr. F Clef.

Then the Clefs jumped onto the keyboard and began to dance and sing.

Mrs. G Clef sang, "On the keyboard my sounds become so bright.

Listen to them as I move from Middle C to the right!"

Mr. F Clef sang, "On the keyboard to the left of Middle C,

is where my musical sounds will be!"

16

Then the musical alphabet, with their instruments in hand,
came marching to the party with their musical band.

"We are not like the regular alphabet that goes from A to Z.
We are the musical alphabet. We go from A to G!"

Then from A to G,
and in perfect harmony,
the alphabet started taking their places
on Grand Staff's musical lines and spaces.

"We are the musical alphabet.
We are the names musical pitches get.
We give names to all the places
on Grand Staff's musical lines and spaces!"

"On our instruments we do the same.
We give musical pitches their musical names.
C, D, E, F, G, A, B!
Do, re, mi, Fa, Sol, la, ti!"

22

Then Grand Staff invited the musical notes. "Look at me," sang Ms. Whole Note.
"I am hollow and round. You can count four beats while I make my musical sound!"
"We are solid with a stem," sang the Quarter Notes. "We make sounds again and aga
Every time you count one beat you will hear one of us again!"

"We are hollow and round," sang the Half Note Twins. "We each have a stem.
You can only count two beats before we make our sounds again!"
"We are solid with flags on top of our stems," declared the Eighth Notes.
"Every time you count to four, eight of us will sound once more!"

Last, Grand Staff invited Father Time and Officer Bar Line.
"It will be our pleasure to give your music four beats per measure!" they sang.
"I will tell the notes to carry their sounds to a count of four!"
declared Father Time.

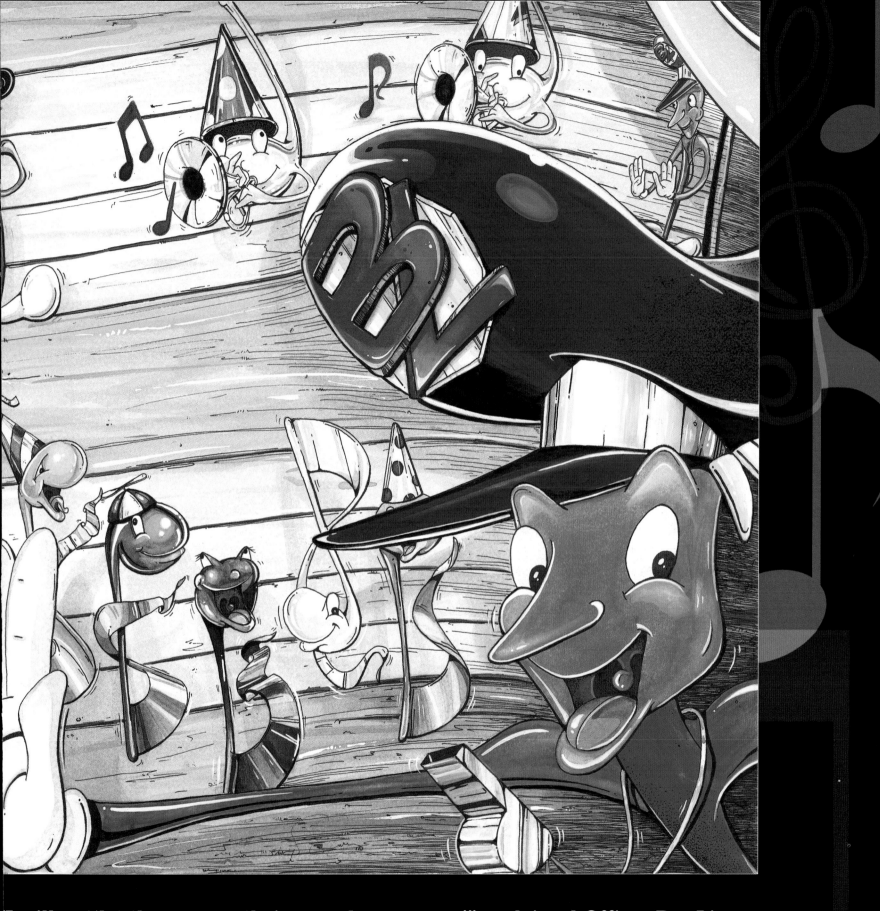

"I will not let them carry their sounds any more!" exclaimed Officer Bar Line.
"Count to four!" ordered Father Time. And the notes began to play.
"Go!" demanded Officer Bar Line. And their music was on its way!

So the party went on and great music was made.
And the talented musicians enjoyed what was played!

Would you like to hear the music they played?
(*Listen to your musical CD!*)

Grand Staff Musical Productions, LLC

www.grandstaffmusic.com

www.musicalcartoons.com

www.kidsmusicdepot.com

"Don't forget to catch me in Grand Staff's next book, *The Dynamics of Music*, in your favorite stores soon!"

Portions of the proceeds from the sales of this book go to the Mr. Holland's Opus Foundation and The VH1 Save the Music Foundation, to foster and promote music education in our schools.

This book is dedicated to Joshua and Jessica Van Schaick

Copyright © 2005 by Grand Staff Musical Productions, LLC

Grand Staff Musical Productions, LLC
13283 S. W. 124th Street
Miami, Florida 33186
(305) 235-2999
www.grandstaffmusic.com
www.musicalcartoons.com
www.kidsmusicdepot.com

A music entertainment and educational resource!

An introduction to music for all ages!

ISBN 0-9765133-0-7

Typeset in Times New Roman and Claredon by Greg Lehman

Pre-press by Phoenix Color Corp.
40 Green Pond Road
Rockaway, NJ 07866

Printed in China

By Mike Singer, Dana Duane Craft and Robert Dante

Stay

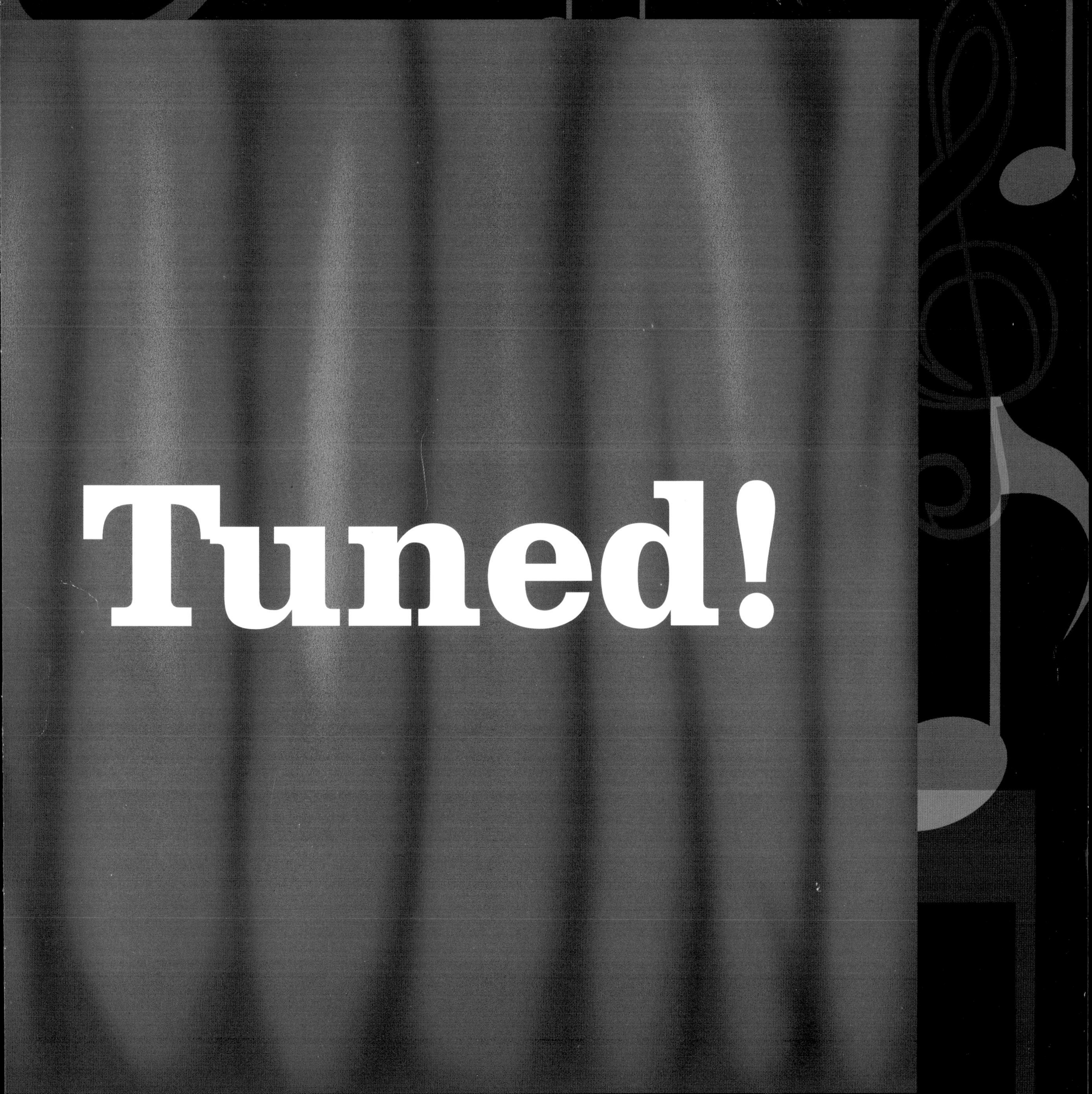
Tuned!